FOCUS ON

RUSSIA AND THE REPUBLICS

Elizabeth Roberts

Evans Brothers Limited

The author and publishers would like to thank the Britain-Russia Centre for all their help in the preparation of this book.

Published by Evans Brothers Limited
2A Portman Mansions
Chiltern Street
London W1M 1LE

Editor Caroline Sheldrick
Design by James Ralton
Map by Hardlines

Printed in Spain by GRAFO, S.A. - Bilbao

ISBN 0 237 60308 X

Acknowledgements

The author and publishers would like to thank the following for permission to reproduce the photographs: Bruce Coleman Limited – cover, contents page, 8 (left) Simon Matthews, 9 (bottom left) Charles Henneghien, 10 (right) Jonathan Wright, 21 (bottom left) Jonathan Wright, 25 (top left) Jeremy Grayson, 26 (left) Hans Reinhard, (right) Rod Williams, 27 (right) Hans Reinhard; Catherine Cooke 15 (left), 21 (top left), 25 (right); Rex Features 10 (left) Andy Hernandez, 12 (right), 30 (right), 31; 23 Copyright © Guinness Publishing Ltd 1989; Robert Harding Picture Library 7 (top left), 8 (right) David B. A. Jones, 11, 15 (right); The Hutchison Library title page, 7 (bottom right), 20 (top) Victoria Juleva, 22 Victoria Juleva 24 Robert Francis; The Imagebank 14 John Bryson; Novosti 9 (bottom right), 21 (right), 28 (right); Oxford Scientific Films 27 (left) Martyn Colbeck; Panos Pictures 9 (top left) Sean Sprague, 13 (right) Sean Sprague, 28 (left) Sean Sprague, 29 (right) Sean Sprague, 30 (right) Heidi Bradner; The Photographers' Library 16 (right); John Massey Stewart 6, 12 (left), 18, 19, 20 (top); Zefa 29 (left).

Cover: View over the Kremlin with (far right) St Basil's Cathedral.

Title Page: This nomadic Chukotka family breeds reindeer. They live in tents. Their territory is on the peninsula in the furthest eastern region of Russia, only a few kilometres from the USA across the Bering Straits.

Opposite: Peaceful musk-ox make the most of brief summer days browsing on the vast Siberian tundra in the north of Russia beyond the Arctic Circle.

Contents

Introducing Russia and the Republics

Russia, also called the Russian Federation, is one of the biggest countries in the world. It stretches over 10,000 kilometres from Europe in the west right across Asia to the Pacific Ocean in the east. Until 1991, Russia was part of an even bigger state called the Union of Soviet Socialist Republics (USSR, or Soviet Union for short). There were 15 Republics in the Soviet Union. They are now all independent.

A vast country

To the north, Russia is bordered by the Arctic Ocean. To the west are the three Baltic states which were once part of the Soviet Union: Estonia, Latvia and Lithuania. To the south of them are Belarus, Ukraine and Moldova. The Caucasus mountain range marks the southern border of Russia. In the south are the three Republics of Georgia, Armenia and Azerbaijan. Beyond the

Caspian Sea, Russia is bordered by Kazakhastan, China and Mongolia. Japan and the USA are Russia's near neighbours in the east. The Ural mountains run like a spine from north to south dividing European Russia from Siberia and the east. Russia has great rivers which run through the vast flat plains. The climate is continental: long hard winters, short springs and hot summers.

Races and rulers

There are 148 million people living in Russia. Another 140 million live in the other 14 former Republics. They are of many different races. In Russia most of the people are Slavs. Next come Turkic peoples such as Tatars.

For many years Russia was part of an empire ruled by the royal family; the emperors were known as Tsars. Then in 1917 the Communists took over. No other political party was allowed. The Communist party was overthrown in August 1991, and an organisation called the Commonwealth of Independent States (CIS) was formed.

The Republics

Baltic states

The three Baltic states of Estonia, Latvia and Lithuania together have a population of about 8.8 million. They never wanted to be part of the Soviet Union. They were independent between 1918 and 1939, but then they were forced to join the USSR. Each has its own language and culture. Lithuanians are Catholics, Estonians are Lutherans, while Latvians are a mixture of both.

Republics in the west

Belarus, Moldova and Ukraine have often been over-run in the past and ruled by invaders. There are over 10 million Belarussians. They speak a language very like Russian, written in the same alphabet. The capital, Minsk, is the headquarters of the Commonwealth of Independent States.

Moldova used to be part of Romania, and most of the people speak Romanian. But some Moldovans on the border with Ukraine are not Romanian, and would like their region to join Ukraine.

Ukraine is about the size of France, with 52 million people. After Russia and Kazakhstan, it is the biggest and richest Republic. Ukrainians speak a language close to Russian. Their capital, Kiev, was the centre of the ancient country of Rus, which existed before modern Russia.

St Andrew's Church stands on a hill overlooking the River Dnieper in Kiev. It was built betweeen 1746-61 by the Italian architect Rastrelli, who designed many of St Petersburg's great buildings.

Caucasian Republics

The three countries near the Caucasus mountains are Georgia, Armenia and Azerbaijan. They are at the crossroads of two continents, Europe and Asia. Georgia is wild and beautiful. The Russian royal family used to spend holidays in spa towns such as Borzhomi, which they developed. There are lovely snowy mountains and pretty vineyards. There has been fighting in Georgia since independence.

Armenia is the world's oldest Christian state. There are 3.3 million Armenians, who are famous for their skill as traders. There are many groups of Armenians who live abroad, and faithfully keep their traditions

A herd of wild horses galloping along a dusty road in Kirgizstan. There are many traditional Kirgiz horseback pursuits, including racing polo (played with a dead goat) and kiss-chase. In the background can be seen the great mountain range of Tien Shan on the border with China.

and language. Armenia is a mountainous country which produces much wine and fruit for export; it has beautiful buildings and excellent building materials.

Azerbaijan has 7 million people, who speak a form of Turkish. It was the world's first great oil-producing area, but reserves are now low. Some oil lies under the waters of the nearby Caspian Sea. Many Armenians used to live in the capital Baku, but they have fled because of fighting. This is because of a violent dispute over an area of land now within the borders of Azerbaijan.

Republics east of the Caspian Sea

East of the Caspian Sea lie the five countries of former Soviet Central Asia. Kazakhstan is the largest, being 2.7 million square kilometres in area with 17 million people. Only a small minority are actually Kazakhs, because many Russians and Ukrainians also live there. In 1944 the ruler Stalin forced groups of Tatars, Germans and other races to go and live there.

The people of Uzbekistan, Kirgizstan, Turkmenistan and Tadzhikistan are of Turkic origin and most are Muslims. Under the Communists they were not allowed to practise their religion. These people were once nomads, ranging with herds of horses, sheep and goats across their vast lands. They lived in tents called *yurts.* Many of these people have had their way of life ruined. The government divided them up by making artificial state boundaries. There have also been man-made environmental disasters: pollution and soil erosion. In these areas there is very poor health care and housing. The economy is also in crisis. It relies on one crop – cotton – to sell abroad.

An Uzbek trader selling pumpkins on a market stall at the Ali bazaar in the capital, Tashkent. Uzbeks grow a lot of produce and the bazaars are always full of fruit and vegetables despite an overdependence on the cotton crop.

Moscow

Moscow, the capital city of Russia, stands on the River Moskva. (Russia was sometimes called 'Muscovy' by visitors long ago.) The city was first developed by Prince Yuri Dolgoruki. He built a fort beside the river in 1147 and named it 'Moskva'. The fort is known as the Kremlin, and Russia's leaders work there to this day.

A view of the Kremlin showing the Saviour gate-tower (with clock face), Ivan the Great bell-tower (two tallest domes), the Cathedrals of the Annunciation, the Archangel Cathedral, and the Cathedral of the Assumption and (far left) the Great Kremlin Palace.

The old centre

Inside the Kremlin there are many beautiful old buildings, including palaces, cathedrals and churches. Outside the Kremlin is Red Square ('red' and 'beautiful' were the same word in old Russian). In it is St Basil's Cathedral, which has multi-coloured onion-shaped domes. Over the centuries, Red Square became a traditional place for public events such as processions and executions. Visitors to the Kremlin museums can see the weapons, carriages and jewels used by the rulers of Russia through the ages.

Nearly nine million people live in Moscow, and many others come as visitors.

St Basil's Cathedral was built between 1555-1561 to celebrate the capture of the Tatar city of Kazan by Tsar Ivan the Terrible. Its patterned multicoloured domes have been compared to turbans or a box of sweets. It is named after a holy fool (Basil) who predicted the evil deeds of Tsar Ivan. Basil was made a saint after he died and is buried next to the church.

A traditional 'onion dome' 18th century Russian Orthodox Christian church with an enormous multi-storey 1930s 'Stalin wedding cake' behind it. Once despised, these Stalin period buildings are now recognised as fine examples of an historical style that should be conserved.

In complete contrast, a 1980s apartment block in Moscow's fastest-growing suburb, named in Russian the "Yugo-zapadnaya" – "southwestern". Despite massive building projects such as this, Moscow's housing problem is acute, because so many people want to live in the capital.

Moscow is a centre of government and the arts. International conferences and trade fairs are held there. The city is 40 kilometres long and 35 wide. The map of Moscow looks like a section cut through a tree trunk: at the centre are the oldest parts, with rings of roads and buildings built more recently round the edge. Some of the prettiest buildings in Moscow were built in the 18th and 19th centuries, and are coloured pale yellow, green or pink.

Modern Moscow

More recently-built streets are wider, and the buildings larger. During the 1930s and 1940s when Stalin ruled, there was a fashion for tall blocks built in tiers. Foreigners call them 'Stalin's wedding cakes'. As the city grew, new roads had to be built so that traffic could avoid the crowded city centre. There are three ring roads around Moscow: the Boulevard ring, the Garden ring and the Moscow Circular Road.

The best way to travel in Moscow is by the underground railway, called the Metro. It has 132 stations, many of them decorated like palaces, with marble walls and floors, bronze statues, wall mosaics and chandeliers. Trains run as often as every 20 seconds in the rush hour.

Towns and cities

Most Russian people live in flats in towns or cities. Moscow is the largest city with nine million people. St Petersburg is next with five million, then Nizhni-Novgorod (known in Soviet times as Gorky), Novosibirsk, and Samara with more than one million each. Nearly 60 per cent of the population now lives in urban areas.

Until very recently, there were no bright advertisements like these on Russian city streets. This new advert for M & M's sweets says: "They melt in your mouth, not in your hand".

Regional contrasts

Russia is vast, so its cities lie in areas with different climates, histories and traditions. Novgorod is in north-west Russia. It was founded in the 9th century by Vikings. In later years, they went south to settle on the banks of the River Dnieper. Their southern settlements became known as 'Rus' after the word for oarsmen – *ruotsi*. By the 12th century, Novgorod was the biggest city in Russia. It has a beautiful cathedral, St Sophia's, finished in AD 1050. Across the other side of the river is the old market arcade and more ancient churches dating back to the 13th century. There are also the remains of the palaces of the Novgorod princes. Like many Russian towns, Novgorod was badly damaged during the Second World War.

In complete contrast, Novosibirsk only developed in 1893, when the famous Trans-Siberian railway arrived at that point to cross the River Ob'. Nearby is an even newer

A 19th century wooden town house from a more leisurely era in a leafy street in Simbirsk, until recently called Ulyanovsk, after Lenin, founder of the former Soviet state.

town, Akademgorodok, a 'science city' founded in the 1950s.

Typical sights

Old towns and cities often have an interesting historical centre, but modern blocks of flats all look much the same. They are usually between nine and twelve storeys high. There is a great housing shortage in Russia, and people have to manage with a small amount of space each. Until very recently most people wanted only to live in a flat and work in town. Now some people see the advantages of the cosy traditional wooden houses with land round them, where vegetables can be grown and a few chickens kept. Food is hard to get in cities.

Many Russian cities were renamed during the Soviet period. Now the old names are coming back. That is not the only change. In Soviet times, there was very little litter or street crime. Now there is a breakdown of law and order, and it is not so safe to go out at night.

St Petersburg

Russia's second biggest city is St Petersburg. It was built on marshy land in the 18th century by Tsar Peter the Great. After the Russian Revolution in 1917, it was named Leningrad after Lenin, the Communist leader who took power after the Tsar was forced to abdicate. St Petersburg is in the north of Russia, near the border with Finland. Its buildings are among the most splendid in the world. It is situated on the River Neva and many of its long streets of Italian-style buildings are on canals. St Petersburg is sometimes called 'the Venice of the North' for this reason.

The Russian alphabet

How would you write MOSKVA (Moscow) in Russian letters?

(You will find the answers on page 32.)

1

▲	●	■
Б	б	b
К	к	k
М	м	m
Т	т	t
З	з	z

2

▲	●	■
Д	д	d
Ф	ф	f
Г	г	g
Л	л	l
Н	н	n
П	п	p
Р	р	r
С	с	s
В	в	v
Й	й	y

3

▲	●	■
Ч	ч	ch
Х	х	kh
Ш	ш	sh
Щ	щ	shch
Ц	ц	ts
Ж	ж	zh
	ъ	soft sign

4

▲	●	■
А	а	a
Я	я	yah
Э	э	eh
Е	е	yeh
Ы	ы	ih
И	и	i(ee)
О	о	oh
Ё	ё	yo
У	у	u(oo)
Ю	ю	yu

1 Russian consonants that look and sound like English
2 Russian consonants that sound like English but look different
3 Russian consonants that look and sound different
4 Vowels

▲ Russian capital letter ● Russian small letter ■ English letter

The 47.5 metre-high Alexander Column in Palace Square, St Petersburg, commemorates the 1812 victory over Napoleon and is named after Tsar Alexander I. The Square is named after the Winter Palace, once the residence of the Tsars and now one of the world's biggest and best art galleries.

Country life

Country life in Russia varies tremendously from region to region. In the far north, people trap animals for fur and keep herds of reindeer. In the east, near Lake Baikal, farmers tend herds of horses and cattle.

Much of the land in Russia is wooded *taiga* or flat, rolling *steppe*. Under the Soviet government, all land belonged to the state. Enormous and inefficient state farms produced sugar-beet, grain, chickens, wool, meat and potatoes. Much that was produced rotted in fields instead of getting to market. Now people want to own land themselves, as they do in the west.

Farming problems

Life in the countryside is often hard; there are few modern conveniences. Many houses and even some hospitals have no running water. Long, cold winters mean that for many months of the year people cannot travel. When the spring rains come, farm machines often get bogged down in the mud. In many parts of Russia the climate is not reliable for growing wheat and other cereals. Some years it is too cold, too wet or too dry, and the crops and animals suffer. The ploughing of fine, sandy soil has caused massive erosion in some areas. The earth

Machinery is hard to keep in good repair – shortages of spares and lack of maintenance facilities often keep tractors in the sheds instead of on the land. This one is in Buryatia, one of Russia's many Autonomous Republics in the far east of Siberia.

Hand-picking potatoes is hard work, but individual plots have traditionally yielded a far greater proportion of Russia's food for their size than the big collective farms.

Fishermen on the Volga River bringing in the catch. Pollution and over-exploitation has threatened the livelihood of many who follow traditional Russian country pursuits, including fishermen and hunters.

blows away and there is nothing left to grow crops in. Towns are far apart, and roads and railways are poor, and there are no modern methods of packaging and distribution to save produce from getting spoiled.

Homes in the country

Village people sometimes live in the traditional old houses. In northern Russia these are wooden *izbas*. Far to the east, in Siberia, the wooden houses have magnificently carved window frames. On Kizhi Island in north-west Russia, there is a collection of beautiful old wooden country churches and houses. Here, visitors can see how Russians used to live.

Many modern farm buildings are crudely made of concrete blocks. Many of the country people were put to death who knew how to build the wooden houses in the early years of Soviet rule. Since then, many country people have lost their will to do things for themselves. They fear that one day they may also be punished.

Russian town dwellers love to travel into the countryside at weekends and for holidays. They spend much of their spare time walking and resting there. Many Russians have a *dacha*: a country cottage. Because land is not scarce in Russia, this is an affordable luxury. A *dacha* is often built of wood, and is sometimes little more than a hut. A favourite Russian pastime in autumn is to go collecting mushrooms and edible fungi in the woods. These can be dried and then used throughout the winter in soups and stews.

These highly-decorated, painted and carved wooden houses are typical of Siberian country style. The harsh climate makes gardening difficult, so this is another way of making the best of your home.

Everyday life

Changing from the old Communist system is very difficult for the Russian people. For 75 years, all aspects of everyday life were controlled by a corrupt state. As a result, standards became very low. Health care was poor. Education was also of a low standard, except for very bright students, chosen by fierce competition, and for the children of the ruling party members. Special schools taught children gifted in mathematics and music. Ordinary children went to schools with few modern facilities or equipment. Learning was generally by repetition or memory, according to a national syllabus. Questions and debate were discouraged.

The family

Childhood has always been a very special time for Russians. Most Russian couples have only one child, so children are treasured and sometimes spoilt. Because of the housing shortage, Russian families often have a *babushka,* or granny, living with them. If they are not lucky enough to have a handy *babushka,* Russian children go at a very early age to be looked after in a nursery and then playschool. This is because most Russian women go out to work as well as looking after their home and family. More than 90 per cent of Russian women are either working or studying. Russian women do many jobs which seem unusual to people in the west, such as road-sweeping or working on building sites. Most doctors and engineers in Russia are women. There is a growing women's movement in Russia; many women have begun to demand more support from Russian men.

Children are treasured in Russia – here are some at nursery school dressed in their best clothes. Many of them are 'only' children – the one child in a family. Most mothers have to go out to work as well as bring up a child, do all the shopping and look after the house.

Alcoholism is still a big problem in Russian everyday life. Many men drink too much, and become violent at home. They lose time at work. Many women also drink too much. Good welfare services in Russia have not been provided. Old people's homes and orphanages are not pleasant places to be in. Charities were banned in the former Soviet Union. Now, once again, people in voluntary societies are starting to provide all kinds of welfare help.

Holidays

Not many Russians can afford to travel abroad, although they are now free to do so. Russia is so enormous that people can take holidays in a different climate and time zone without leaving the country. Many people used to take their holidays in places belonging to their trade union. Children used to go to 'Young Pioneer' camps, run by the state, where they enjoyed outdoor activities. A typical Russian holiday is one spent at a health centre or spa. Health resorts date back to the 19th century, and often have good sports facilities.

A typical Russian street scene: these people are looking at little advertisements for accommodation, or goods or services. They are handwritten on pieces of paper with a fringe of tear-off strips giving the telephone number to contact the seller or person offering a flat-swap.

Shopping in the markets is more expensive than the shops, but often it is the only way to find meat, fruit or vegetables. The Russian letters printed above the entrance to the bazaar spell "Ovoshchi" – vegetables.

Special days

The first day of school is an important day for a Russian child. Children put on a white apron or a white shirt, and take flowers for their teacher. Getting married also has its special rituals and church weddings are now popular. There are also 'wedding palaces' where couples take civil vows in front of an official. Then the happy couple will often go and lay flowers on the local war memorial.

Russian words

There is no Russian word for 'privacy' but there are many useful words for which there is no exact English equivalent. For instance:

glasnost	speaking out, publicity, openness
perestroika	rebuilding, restructuring
poshlost	vulgarity, cheapness, showing off
toska	a sad, yearning feeling
sobornost	togetherness

Power and industry

Russia is very rich in natural resources. It produces energy from coal, oil, natural gas, wood and peat. Water power and nuclear power are also important. However, there is neglect and waste at all stages of power production. No attempt has been made to charge the user (in homes or industry) a price which covers costs. There are huge price rises of up to 600 per cent planned.

There are vast areas of woodland in Russia: this forest road with timber stacked on either side is on the Russian-Finnish border.

Fuel for export

There has always been the problem in Russia of getting power across vast distances. A pipeline was built in the 1980s to take natural gas from Siberia to western Europe. They also export coal and oil, which have to be removed from difficult sites in Siberia. Coal miners and oilfield workers have asked for more rewards for their labour, such as a share of the foreign currency earned.

Power for Russia

Some of Russia's electricity is provided by water power. A dam 1.5 kilometres long across the Volga River at Volgograd turns 22 turbines and produces 11.5 billion kilowatt hours of electricity every year. Since 1958, Russia has also produced energy from nuclear power stations. Russia still has vast pine forests which provide timber for housing and fuel for stoves.

Manufacturing

Russia also has great reserves of gold, diamonds, iron ore and many other minerals

This gas pipeline runs from Siberia to Western Europe. Sales of natural gas bring in much-needed foreign currency.

Heavy industry, such as this steel foundry in Togliatti on the Volga, needs to modernise itself to compete in world markets and conform to modern safety standards.

Russian cars have always been in short supply, because the system was not geared to produce goods for the consumer. This bright yellow model is on a 2km long production line in Togliatti.

needed for modern industry. Over the years, the government encouraged the development of heavy industry, such as making steel for ships, submarines and tanks. Less effort went into the production of consumer goods: items like cameras and hairdryers. These were often imported cheaply from other Communist countries such as East Germany and Czechoslovakia. Russia has to start learning to make consumer goods or else import them at the world market prices. Another problem is that the Russian currency, the rouble, was not part of the world currency system. After the Soviet system collapsed, the rouble lost even its internal value. People's savings became worthless. By the time the Soviet regime ended in 1991, industry was producing far less. To earn foreign currency Russia has to sell goods abroad, and foreign trade was down by 38 per cent that year.

Warning to the world

Attitudes to nuclear power have changed all over the world since a reactor blew up at Chernobyl in the Ukraine. Radioactivity was released over a wide area. Many people risked their lives to bring the power station back under control and encase it in a concrete jacket. It looks as though about 10,000 people, including many children, will die as a direct result of the accident, which happened in 1986. Many more will be born with severe defects caused by the exposure of their parents to radiation. People cannot live and crops cannot be grown on land within a wide circle of the scene of the accident. People in St Petersburg have urged their local authorities to close down a reactor of similar design which has released clouds of radioactive gas.

Culture and food

One of the most striking things about Russia is the importance attached to culture. The Russian word *nekulturny,* which means uncultured, is a crushing word of abuse. People fill football stadiums to watch football, but they have also been known to fill them to listen to poetry. Serious authors are respected both by their readers and the government in a way that is difficult for us to understand.

Russian masterpieces

Until the 19th century, Russian literature and music were not widely known abroad. This all changed when a number of writers and composers produced a series of masterpieces. There were novels such as *War and Peace* by Tolstoy, plays such as *The Cherry Orchard* by Chekhov and great pieces of music such as the ballet score *The Sleeping Beauty* written by Tchaikovsky. After the Revolution there was a clampdown on new ideas. The Soviet government banned many books and films. Under *glasnost,* the policy of openness introduced by Mikhail Gorbachev in 1985, things improved. This has continued and now many books and films which were banned for years can be enjoyed again in Russia.

The unearthly beauty of dancers from the famous Maryinsky (known as the Kirov in Soviet times) ballet company of St Petersburg in their traditional white dresses.

Folk culture

Folk art – from choral singing to fairy-tales – is a treasured part of Russian culture. A favourite fairy-tale character is Ivan Durachok. He is a simple lad who escapes death and triumphs over wickedness through his innocence. Every Russian child shivers at the name of Baba-Yaga. Baba-Yaga is a witch who eats children.

Stage and screen

Some of the greatest film-makers in the history of cinema were born in Russia, including Eisenstein and Tarkovsky. The former Soviet Union had more than half the cinemas in the world. There are many video-salons too, even in small villages. Everyone in Russia watches television and every town has its own theatre.

Another favourite form of entertainment is the circus. Russian circuses with clowns and performing animals are famous all over the world. Russian opera singers are amongst the best there are, and so are their ballet dancers. Many of the greatest ballets were created in Russia.

Chess
One of the national passions is chess. There are millions of club players. In parks and halls you can see players of all ages deeply engrossed in the game. Russian grandmaster Anatoly Karpov was unbeaten for years, and Baku-born Armenian Gary Kasparov is still regarded by many as the world's greatest player.

A Russian meal
Russians take eating and drinking seriously. Feasting and having friends to one's house are an important part of Russian life. Such occasions are not formal – people will often arrive bringing an extra unexpected guest if they happen to meet them on the way. Russians do not have drinks before a meal. They sit down to table straight away. A Russian meal begins with *zakuski*, an array of little cold dishes laid out on the table. These can include smoked fish, cold meat, pickled mushrooms and cucumbers, spring onions and the black or red fish eggs we call caviar. There will be sliced brown or white bread and ice-cold vodka. This is drunk a small glass at a time, tossed back in one gulp. After *zakuski* there may be soup, like *borshch* (beetroot) or *shchi* (cabbage). Then there may be meat or fish with potatoes, followed by stewed fruit (*compot*) or ice-cream.

Favourite foods

Ice-cream is very popular in Russia and is very delicious. It can be bought from street sellers in summer and winter. In Moscow it is claimed that 170 tonnes are eaten every day of the year! Other traditional takeaways include *kvas*, a non-alcoholic drink made from rye bread.

Bread is a vital part of the Russian diet and people choose it carefully like other people might choose wine. In many bread shops there is a little flat spoon on a chain used by people to tap a loaf to see if it is baked to their taste. A book is provided for complaints and suggestions.

Russian cabbage pie
Preparation time: 30 minutes
Cooking time: 30 minutes
INGREDIENTS (Generous quantities for 4)
white cabbage 350 grams (14 oz)
1 medium onion 125 grams (5 oz)
butter 50 grams (2 oz)
2 hard-boiled eggs
1 beaten egg (to brush top of pie)
ready-made frozen puff pastry 350 grams (14 oz)
salt
freshly ground black pepper

METHOD
For cabbage filling
Cut cabbage into thin strips and remove hard core. Slice onion. Hard boil 2 eggs. Meanwhile, melt butter in frying pan and cook onion gently until soft and golden. Boil kettle and pour boiling water over sliced cabbage. Drain and sprinkle with salt. Add blanched cabbage to onion and continue to cook gently in butter for 10 minutes until soft and golden.

To make the pie
Grease a 21cm (8 inch) pie dish and line with half the puff pastry. Cut up hard-boiled eggs. Mix eggs, cabbage and onion in a mixing bowl and season with salt and pepper. Lay mixture on pastry base in pie dish. Cover with rest of pastry and brush with beaten egg. Cook for 20 minutes in pre-heated oven at Gas Mark 7 (220C/425F). Turn down to Mark 4 (180C/350F) for a further 10 minutes: take out of oven, let cool for 15 minutes.

Religion and tradition

Religious belief was seen as an old-fashioned superstition by the Communist government. They tried to stop people following their religions. However, there are still many religions, including Christianity and Islam, surviving in Russia and the Republics today.

The Orthodox Church

The traditional religion of Russia since AD 988 has been Orthodox Christianity. The old heart of the Russian Orthodox church is the Troitse-Sergeyeva Lavra, near Moscow. Here pilgrims come to worship at the many beautiful old churches. There is also a theological college where priests are trained.

Russian churches are ornate inside and out. They have onion-shaped domes often painted gold. Inside, they are highly decorated with pictures of the lives of the saints and Jesus and the Virgin Mary. It is rather dark and mysterious inside a Russian church, lit mostly by flickering candles and with the scent of incense and beeswax in the air.

There are no chairs in a Russian church. Services are long, and people enter and move around while the service is going on. The only music in the Orthodox church is unaccompanied part-singing of hypnotic beauty; Russian choir singers often have very deep bass voices. Russian priests have long beards and tall black hats. A parish priest has to be married, so that he can better understand the problems of all members of his congregation. Under Soviet rule churches were forbidden to do charitable work. Now they organize help for the poor and sick.

(Far left) A Russian Orthodox priest in his ornate robes in front of a richly-decorated gold altar screen.

(Left) This 12th century icon shows the patron saint of Russia, St George (mounted centre) and his adventures. It can now be seen in the Russian Museum in St Petersburg.

Easter

The most important festival in the Orthodox church is Easter. On Easter eve, there is a midnight service. On Easter Day, you say 'Christ is Risen!' instead of 'Good morning', and people reply 'He is risen indeed'. There are special dishes to eat at Easter and people decorate hard-boiled eggs. In the last century, the Tsar of Russia used to order beautiful eggs made of precious stones and enamel to give to his family from a famous St Petersburg jeweller called Fabergé.

A Russian Orthodox priest blessing Easter cakes called "kulichi". Easter is the high point of the Christian year especially in Russia.

Tatar worshippers in a mosque in Kazan, an ancient city founded in the 13th century.

Tradition

Every country has its own traditions and superstitions – and Russia is no exception. For instance, it is considered bad luck to shake hands or greet a guest while standing on the threshold, or doorway, of a house. The guest must either come right in or you must go out to meet him. It is also considered bad luck to turn back for something once you have started a journey. Before leaving it is the custom to sit down for a moment of silence. Perhaps this has something to do with the idea that your soul is separate from your body and must have a chance to get back into your body before you leave.

Ancient rituals persist in some Russian villages; this is 'tossing the bear' – the winner of a ritual trial of strength.

Other religions

There are estimated to be 50 million Muslims, followers of the Islamic religion, in Russia and the Republics. They mainly live in the Central Asian republics such as Uzbekistan. But there is a significant minority within Russia itself who are Muslims, such as the Tatars of the Middle Volga and Urals.

Many Buryats in Siberia are Buddhists. Other tribes in Russia are shamanist, worshipping spirits of earth and water. There is a history of persecution of Jews in Russia. They have always had their religion noted on their passports. Many have emigrated to the USA and Israel, but two million or so remain.

Travel

Transport is crucial to everyday life in Russia. Travellers have to overcome vast distances, a harsh climate and hostile terrain. The Trans-Siberian railway, for instance, runs from Moscow to Vladivostok on the Pacific coast across 9,298 kilometres of land. The journey takes eight days; the train only stops for about 20 minutes at each of the 91 stops along the way. Until very recently Russians were not free to travel wherever they liked, even inside their own country. A passport to travel abroad was issued only for one particular journey, then it had to be handed back. This limit on travel went back to before Soviet times.

Russian trains are wider than other Western European trains: passengers on the Trans-Siberian express can while away the days sitting in the dining car.

By rail and air

Russian trains are wider than most European ones and there is an attendant in each carriage on sleeper trains who keeps a *samovar* of tea on the go. When visiting Russia, it is a good idea to take the sleeper train overnight from Moscow to St Petersburg, which saves time for sightseeing. In recent times, an alternative route has been added to part of the old Trans-Siberian railway, called the Baikal-Amur mainline – or BAM for short. This line runs further north than the old route, which runs very close to the Chinese border.

Flying is very often the best way of getting from place to place in Russia. The old Soviet airline, Aeroflot, was the biggest in the world. It linked 3,600 towns and cities within Russia and the Republics. Now, Aeroflot carries 112 million passengers a year, but they are frequently delayed because of a shortage of fuel. Planes are often diverted hundreds of kilometres in search of fuel supplies.

There is no smoking or alcohol allowed on Aeroflot flights within Russia and the Republics, and the meal is always a chicken leg. Alternative airlines are planned within Russia and the Republics, such as Russian International and Air Rossiya.

By road

Road transport is the poor relation in the Russian transport system. It is difficult and expensive for Russians to buy a car, and there are very few spare parts on sale for when a car goes wrong. Petrol stations are few and far between, and they do not always have petrol. The lorries on Russian roads are often old and worn out by the long distances and poor road surfaces they have to travel, and the heavy loads they carry. Many officials in Moscow have the use of a car and driver. Roads in Moscow are enormously wide and the distances within the city also very great.

Space travel

Russia and the Republics were pioneers in Space travel. They launched the first artificial satellite, called *Sputnik* ('traveller') from Russia in 1957. The first manned Space flight was made by Russian cosmonaut Yuri Gagarin in 1961, and the first Space walk was made by Alexei Leonov in 1965. The first prototype manned Space station was *Salyut 1* (1971) and the record for living in Space (365 days) was set by Vladimir Titov and Musa Manarov in 1990.

Russia and the Republics have to decide on the future of the Space programme. Money is now short, and Space scientists are trying to find ways to earn valuable foreign currency. The European Space Agency and NASA (of the USA) are interested in joint ventures with the Russians. Some possible projects involve satellite communications for radio and TV, prospecting from the air for natural resources, watching for damage to the Earth and its atmosphere, and making new materials and medicines in Space.

World record holders for travelling in Space, Vladimir Titov (left) and Musa Manarov (with moustache, right).

Sergei Krikalev was orbiting the Earth in a Space station when the Soviet Union ended. He had been in Space for 11 months before a Soyuz TM13 could be launched to bring him down. In 1992, Space launches were cut by 50 per cent in order to save money.

Some staggering statistics

1 There are 11 time zones in Russia and the Republics. So when it is 7.00pm on Tuesday in Moscow, it is midnight in Lake Baikal and 5.00am in Cape Deznev on Wednesday.

2 The boundaries of Russia and the Republics are 60,000 kilometres long. St Petersburg is closer to Cape Town in South Africa than it is to Vladivostok in eastern Siberia. Russia stretches half-way round our planet.

3 The BAM railway crosses seven mountain ranges, has 3,700 bridges and experiences an average of 2,000 earthquakes a year.

4 Every year 2,400 million people use the Moscow metro.

5 At the closest points, Russia is only 4 km from Japan and 5.4 km from the USA.

Russian winter

Winter is the season when Russia is at its most Russian. Snow begins to fall in November, the rivers freeze and soon the whole countryside looks like a fairy-tale picture. Long icicles hang from the eaves of the buildings. Sometimes, droplets of moisture freeze as they fall through the air and sparkle like tinsel in the dark. In parts of Russia winter can be unbelievably cold.

Coping with the cold

In Siberia, temperatures as low as -70°C below freezing have been recorded. At these very low temperatures, tyres burst and engines have to be kept running all day and night to prevent the oil in them freezing.

Breathing in becomes quite interesting; the little hairs in your nostrils freeze. You can get frostbite if you leave your gloves off for more than minute. Despite all this, Russians prefer their winter to be a proper one with lots of ice and snow. They become quite upset if it thaws unexpectedly during a mild spell. There is a practical reason for this: crops suffer if the blanket of snow protecting them melts and then re-freezes. Melted snow which re-freezes is also more slippery and dangerous to walk on. Russian homes and offices are kept very cosy and

Still beauty on the frozen River Neva in St Petersburg, as the setting winter sun reflects in the palace windows.

Making holes in the ice is not only for fishermen: here, Russian housewives break the ice to do the clothes washing in Suzdal, one of the best-preserved of the so-called 'Golden Ring' of old Russian towns north-east of Moscow.

warm in winter. Russian buildings have double windows and padded doors to keep out draughts.

In Russia, it is the strict custom to take off your winter coat and hat when going to the office or visiting a concert hall, theatre, restaurant or museum. There are special racks provided in the entrance to buildings, and an attendant takes coats and hats and hangs them up. In exchange, they give you a little numbered plastic tag to help find the right ones when you leave again.

Winter sports

Russian children look nearly round when they go out to play in their winter coat, boots, hat and scarf. Tobogganing is popular, and so are cross-country skiing, ice hockey and skating. In winter, rivers freeze over even in the middle of big towns and cities like Moscow and Kiev. People walk out on the ice and make a hole and sit and fish through the hole. Others swim all the year round in the cold water: they belong to the 'Walrus Club'.

Clearing the snow

Because the snow falls from time to time all through the winter, from November to March, there are different machines working all the time to keep the streets clear for pedestrians and traffic. Russian drivers keep a little plastic scraper inside their car to keep the windows clear. As they drive along, frost forms inside the windows and makes it difficult to see out.

There are many weird and wonderful machines designed to clear away snow from Russian streets. This one is called a 'lobster' because of its claw-shaped scoops in front.

Wildlife

The wildlife of Russia is as rich and varied as the landscape of this vast country. In the north, there is the almost bare, flat band of arctic tundra, where the soil is frozen. In the south, there are huge areas of *taiga*, or forests. The rolling *steppes*, or grasslands, stretch from central Russia to the Ural mountains.

Animals in the wild

Russia is famous for its fur-bearing animals. The most impressive of these is the brown bear, standing more than three metres tall. Brown bears like to eat honey and they live in the forest. Wolves and foxes also live in or near the forest. Wolves hunt in family groups, or packs, with a leader. Travellers in Russia used to tell tales of being followed on their sledge by wolves. They thought the wolves would kill and eat them if they fell off. Man in his turn has hunted fur-bearing animals for their valuable pelts. The rarest big cat in Russia is the Siberian tiger; only about 200 are left. Other beautiful Russian mammals include the sable, beaver, marten and ermine.

There are great herds of deer, including elks, in the *taiga*. Elks are very big – 2.3 metres high and 3 metres long – and browse on green shoots and water plants in swampy areas. Even in the forests around Moscow there are elks to be seen, with their enormous branching antlers.

The bear is Russia's national symbol, and is associated in folklore with kindness and wisdom. Real bears can be less cuddly than they look.

A young, female Siberian tiger.

A group of Baikal seals basking in the sunshine.

Birds and fish

If you fly to Moscow, the first birds you will see when you land at Moscow airport are the grey hooded crows. Each habitat has its own typical bird population: in the arctic north, there are puffins, cormorants and geese; in the forests, owls, cuckoos, grouse, tits and woodpeckers; in the mountains, vultures and eagles.

Fish found around Russia's shores and in the lakes and rivers include salmon, sturgeon, herring, roach, carp and bream. Crabs are also found in great numbers off the shores of Kamchatka in Siberia. They are processed and tinned for export.

Conservation

Russians have become very worried about the damage done to the environment by industrial pollution, causing wildlife to suffer. Sometimes marshes have been drained to make more land for farming. This means that many wading birds and waterfowl have lost their homes. Factories and big new towns create harmful waste, which spoils the lakes and rivers for fish. When large dams are built, planners now put in a special channel so that fish can swim upstream in the spring to lay their eggs.

There are dozens of nature reserves in Russia, such as the Barguzin State Nature Reserve on the shores of Lake Baikal in Siberia. This huge area of 2,632 square kilometres contains more than 600 species of flowering plants, 30 species of mammals, including the unique freshwater Baikal seal, reptiles, amphibians and birds.

Plant life

Russia also has fascinating trees and flowers. Russian silver birches seem straighter and whiter than those in western Europe. In the Caucasus there are rare pines and oaks found nowhere else in the world. The vast Russian forests are mostly pine and larch. Timber is an important resource.

Russian silver -birch trees.

Rivers, lakes and mountains

Rivers have played an important part in the development of Russia. In the earliest times, they provided the only long-distance transport system. Even today, it is possible to go by boat direct from Moscow to five seas: north to the Baltic and White Seas and south to the Caspian, Black and Azov Seas. Today, some of Russia's thousands of rivers are also used for irrigation, in industry and for making electricity.

Rivers east and west

In the west, the four most important rivers are the Dnieper and the Don which flow from the Moscow region south to the Black Sea, the Dvina which flows north to the Baltic and the Volga which flows to the Caspian. You may have heard of a famous old Russian folk song called 'Song of the Volga Boatmen'. This was the song the men sang as they pulled their boat along the river. East of the Ural mountains there are four great rivers: the Ob' (the fourth longest river in the world), the Irtysh, the Yenisei and the Lena. All four run north towards the Arctic Circle. In the far east, the river Amur flows into the Pacific Ocean.

Farmers with hay on the shores of the great freshwater Lake Baikal in Siberia. Russia has thousands of rivers and lakes, and farmers often move their crops and livestock by barge.

Barges make their way slowly along the River Volga, one of Russia's great waterways, where it looks as wide as a sea.

A beautiful valley in the western Caucasus.

The highest peaks

The mountains in Russia lie round the edge of the country, except for the Urals which run from north to south down the middle of Russia like a spine. The Caucasus mountains in the south are the border between Russia and the Republics of Georgia and Armenia. In the far east are the mountain ranges of Siberia: the Altai, Sayan, Kuznetsky Alatau and Tuva ranges. The zone around Lake Baikal is also mountainous. Mount Belukha is the highest mountain in the Altai region, at 4,506 metres, rising with a sheer wall of ice and snow. There are many active volcanoes in the vast Kamchatka peninsula in the North Pacific region, including Mount Kluchev at 4,750 metres, one of the world's highest. The Ural mountains are very rich in minerals including iron, copper and gold. Elsewhere in Siberia, silver and platinum are mined. Semi-precious stones such as malachite, jasper and porphyry come from the Altai.

Cows grazing on the edge of Lake Baikal, Siberia. The clear blue waters contain over 2000 plant and animal species, most of them unique to the lake. One special fish called the golomyanka lives 1-1.5km deep, and dissolves into a blob of oil if it is brought to the surface.

There are hundreds of lakes in Russia, but Lake Baikal in Siberia is unique. Twenty per cent of all the fresh water in the whole world is in this enormous lake. The lake is 640 kilometres long and 80 wide, making it the biggest freshwater lake in the world. It is also the oldest – 25 million years old. There are hundreds of species of animals and plants in Lake Baikal that are not found elsewhere in the world, including freshwater seals and seacows. But pollution from factories now threatens the survival of these rare creatures.

Russia and the world

Russia is still a military superpower. It has emerged from the collapse of the Soviet Union with a great arsenal of nuclear weapons and an army of nearly four million. This military power was bought at great cost, however. In some parts of the country, people suffer from lack of basic amenities. Even hospitals may not have sewerage or hot water. There are shortages of basic health-care items such as splints and bandages, and few painkillers and other necessary drugs.

Recent history

Russia is surrounded by countries which for many years it dominated through fear. The Baltic states of Lithuania, Latvia and Estonia were taken into the Soviet empire against their will. Poland, Romania and Czechoslovakia were ruled for many years by governments controlled from Moscow. Then in 1985, economists made clear to the head of the Soviet Union, Mikhail Gorbachev, that his country was doomed unless changes were made. Although

A crowd in Moscow demonstrating after the coup that overthrew Mikhail Gorbachev in August 1991. They are protesting against the Communist 'old guard' which tried to retake control of the government by force.

Russian troops occupied most of Eastern Europe for 45 years, but now they have agreed to leave. There are problems awaiting them when they get home, such as a lack of housing and alternative employment.

Gorbachev introduced free speech (*glasnost*), his attempts at reform (*perestroika*) did not work. He wanted Russia to stay Communist. Russia needed proper laws to help build business at home and trade abroad. Laws were needed to allow peasants to own the land they worked on. Gorbachev struggled

Boris Yeltsin (centre, with megaphone), campaigning in Moscow for the Russian presidency in June 1991.

on for six years; he was popular abroad because he wanted change, but unpopular at home because these changes never happened. The old Soviet Union fell apart in 1991.

The new President of Russia, Boris Yeltsin, is the first Russian leader in history to be elected. He has a very difficult task ahead of him. He must help Russians repair the ruined magnificence of their country.

Recovery

Since the collapse of Soviet power there has been a 35 per cent rise in crime in Moscow and St Petersburg. The old Soviet Union was a tightly-regulated society, although there was widespread corruption. Officials were used to being bribed, for instance.

One of the many things Russia needs is a properly trained civil service. Business in the western sense of buying and selling things for a living, has been illegal in Russia for seventy years. Many Russians do not understand the idea of honest trading. Before 1917, however, Russia was one of the fastest-growing economies in the world. With a democratically-elected government, the rule of law and a free market it might be so again. The rich countries of the world, such as the USA and the European Community, have promised to help Russia recover. The International Monetary Fund (IMF) is helping the Russians to make their currency convertible. That is, they will be able to exchange roubles for other world currencies, such as the lira, Deutsche Mark, dollar or pound. This move is important for free trade.

The Russian Revolution

In 1917 the Bolshevik Party, led by Lenin, seized power in Russia. Their stated aims were 'peace, freedom and bread'. The Tsar of Russia was exiled to the Urals and later murdered there with his family.

The Russian Revolution was unique because it did not just transfer power from one group in society to another. It was an attempt to change the very nature of people and of society.

Many of the ideals behind the Soviet system were set out by Karl Marx, a German philosopher. Marx said that society should expect 'from each according to his ability' and should provide 'to each according to his needs'. But in Soviet Russia many millions of people were killed to further this belief.

Index and summary

Answer to question on page 11
MOCKBA

Area of Russia:	17.1 million square kilometres
Population:	148 million
Capital:	Moscow
Main towns:	St Petersburg, Nizhni-Novgorod, Novosibirsk, Samara, Omsk, Rostov-on-Don, Ekaterinburg, Volgograd, Chelyabinsk, Kazan, Perm, Ufa
Main exports:	Oil, natural gas, timber, furs, vodka, coal, minerals, diamonds, gold
Main imports:	Machinery and equipment, consumer goods, rubber, coffee, cocoa beans
Main crops:	Wheat, barley, maize, sunflower, rye, oats, sugar-beet, flax, potatoes
Highest point:	Mount Elbrus 5,642 metres
Longest river:	Ob'
Official language:	Russian
Currency:	100 kopeks to 1 rouble
National airline:	Aeroflot